THIS BOOK AND THESE EPIC HIGH THOUGHTS BELONG TO

★ MY EPIC HIGH THOUGHTS ABOUT LIFE ★

★ MY EPIC HIGH THOUGHTS ABOUT LIFE ★

★ MY EPIC HIGH THOUGHTS ABOUT LIFE ★

★ MY EPIC HIGH THOUGHTS ABOUT LIFE ★

★ MY EPIC HIGH THOUGHTS ABOUT LIFE ★

★ MY EPIC HIGH THOUGHTS ABOUT LIFE ★

★ MY EPIC HIGH THOUGHTS ABOUT LIFE ★

✹ MY EPIC HIGH THOUGHTS ABOUT LIFE ✹

★ MY EPIC HIGH THOUGHTS ABOUT LIFE ★

★ MY EPIC HIGH THOUGHTS ABOUT LiFE ★

★ MY EPIC HIGH THOUGHTS ABOUT LIFE ★

★ MY EPIC HIGH THOUGHTS ABOUT LIFE ★

★ MY EPIC HIGH THOUGHTS ABOUT LIFE ★

✻ MY EPIC HIGH THOUGHTS ABOUT LIFE ✻

★ MY EPIC HIGH THOUGHTS ABOUT LIFE ★

★ MY EPIC HIGH THOUGHTS ABOUT LIFE ★

★ MY EPIC HIGH THOUGHTS ABOUT LIFE ★

★ MY EPIC HIGH THOUGHTS ABOUT LIFE ★

★ MY EPIC HIGH THOUGHTS ABOUT LIFE ★

★ MY EPIC HIGH THOUGHTS ABOUT LIFE ★

★ MY EPIC HIGH THOUGHTS ABOUT LIFE ★

★ MY EPIC HIGH THOUGHTS ABOUT LIFE ★

✱ MY EPIC HIGH THOUGHTS ABOUT LIFE ✱

★ MY EPIC HIGH THOUGHTS ABOUT LIFE ★

✻ MY EPIC HIGH THOUGHTS ABOUT LIFE ✻

★ MY EPIC HIGH THOUGHTS ABOUT LIFE ★

★ MY EPIC HIGH THOUGHTS ABOUT LIFE ★

★ MY EPIC HIGH THOUGHTS ABOUT LIFE ★

★ MY EPIC HIGH THOUGHTS ABOUT LIFE ★

★ MY EPIC HIGH THOUGHTS ABOUT LIFE ★

★ MY EPIC HIGH THOUGHTS ABOUT LIFE ★

★ MY EPIC HIGH THOUGHTS ABOUT LIFE ★

★ MY EPIC HIGH THOUGHTS ABOUT LIFE ★

★ MY EPIC HIGH THOUGHTS ABOUT LIFE ★

★ MY EPIC HIGH THOUGHTS ABOUT LIFE ★

★ MY EPIC HIGH THOUGHTS ABOUT LIFE ★

★ MY EPIC HIGH THOUGHTS ABOUT LIFE ★

★ MY EPIC HIGH THOUGHTS ABOUT LIFE ★

★ MY EPIC HIGH THOUGHTS ABOUT LIFE ★

✷ MY EPIC HIGH THOUGHTS ABOUT LIFE ✷

★ MY EPIC HIGH THOUGHTS ABOUT LIFE ★

★ MY EPIC HIGH THOUGHTS ABOUT LIFE ★

✷ MY EPIC HIGH THOUGHTS ABOUT LIFE ✷

★ MY EPIC HIGH THOUGHTS ABOUT LIFE ★

★ MY EPIC HIGH THOUGHTS ABOUT LIFE ★

★ MY EPIC HIGH THOUGHTS ABOUT LIFE ★

★ MY EPIC HIGH THOUGHTS ABOUT LIFE ★

★ MY EPIC HIGH THOUGHTS ABOUT LIFE ★

★ MY EPIC HIGH THOUGHTS ABOUT LIFE ★

★ MY EPIC HIGH THOUGHTS ABOUT LIFE ★

★ MY EPIC HIGH THOUGHTS ABOUT LIFE ★

★ MY EPIC HIGH THOUGHTS ABOUT LIFE ★

★ MY EPIC HIGH THOUGHTS ABOUT LIFE ★

★ MY EPIC HIGH THOUGHTS ABOUT LIFE ★

★ MY EPIC HIGH THOUGHTS ABOUT LIFE ★

★ MY EPIC HIGH THOUGHTS ABOUT LIFE ★

✷ MY EPIC HIGH THOUGHTS ABOUT LIFE ✷

★ MY EPIC HIGH THOUGHTS ABOUT LIFE ★

★ MY EPIC HIGH THOUGHTS ABOUT LIFE ★

★ MY EPIC HIGH THOUGHTS ABOUT LIFE ★

★ MY EPIC HIGH THOUGHTS ABOUT LIFE ★

★ MY EPIC HIGH THOUGHTS ABOUT LIFE ★

★ MY EPIC HIGH THOUGHTS ABOUT LIFE ★

✳ **MY EPIC HIGH THOUGHTS ABOUT LIFE** ✳

✶ MY EPIC HIGH THOUGHTS ABOUT LIFE ✶

★ MY EPIC HIGH THOUGHTS ABOUT LIFE ★

★ MY EPIC HIGH THOUGHTS ABOUT LIFE ★

★ MY EPIC HIGH THOUGHTS ABOUT LIFE ★

★ MY EPIC HIGH THOUGHTS ABOUT LIFE ★

★ MY EPIC HIGH THOUGHTS ABOUT LIFE ★

★ MY EPIC HIGH THOUGHTS ABOUT LIFE ★

★ MY EPIC HIGH THOUGHTS ABOUT LIFE ★

★ MY EPIC HIGH THOUGHTS ABOUT LIFE ★

★ MY EPIC HIGH THOUGHTS ABOUT LIFE ★

★ MY EPIC HIGH THOUGHTS ABOUT LIFE ★

✹ MY EPIC HIGH THOUGHTS ABOUT LIFE ✹

✸ MY EPIC HIGH THOUGHTS ABOUT LIFE ✸

★ MY EPIC HIGH THOUGHTS ABOUT LIFE ★

★ MY EPIC HIGH THOUGHTS ABOUT LIFE ★

★ MY EPIC HIGH THOUGHTS ABOUT LIFE ★

★ MY EPIC HIGH THOUGHTS ABOUT LIFE ★

★ MY EPIC HIGH THOUGHTS ABOUT LIFE ★

★ MY EPIC HIGH THOUGHTS ABOUT LIFE ★

★ MY EPIC HIGH THOUGHTS ABOUT LIFE ★

★ MY EPIC HIGH THOUGHTS ABOUT LIFE ★

★ MY EPIC HIGH THOUGHTS ABOUT LIFE ★

★ MY EPIC HIGH THOUGHTS ABOUT LIFE ★

★ MY EPIC HIGH THOUGHTS ABOUT LIFE ★

✺ MY EPIC HIGH THOUGHTS ABOUT LIFE ✺

★ MY EPIC HIGH THOUGHTS ABOUT LIFE ★

★ MY EPIC HIGH THOUGHTS ABOUT LIFE ★

★ MY EPIC HIGH THOUGHTS ABOUT LIFE ★

★ MY EPIC HIGH THOUGHTS ABOUT LIFE ★

★ MY EPIC HIGH THOUGHTS ABOUT LIFE ★

★ MY EPIC HIGH THOUGHTS ABOUT LIFE ★

★ MY EPIC HIGH THOUGHTS ABOUT LIFE ★

★ MY EPIC HIGH THOUGHTS ABOUT LIFE ★

★ MY EPIC HIGH THOUGHTS ABOUT LIFE ★

✱ MY EPIC HIGH THOUGHTS ABOUT LIFE ✱

★ MY EPIC HIGH THOUGHTS ABOUT LIFE ★

★ MY EPIC HIGH THOUGHTS ABOUT LIFE ★

✴ MY EPIC HIGH THOUGHTS ABOUT LIFE ✴

★ MY EPIC HIGH THOUGHTS ABOUT LIFE ★

_____

_____

_____

_____

_____

_____

_____

_____

_____

_____

_____

_____

_____

_____

_____

_____

_____

_____

_____

_____

_____

_____

_____

_____

_____

Made in United States
North Haven, CT
26 October 2022

25924745R00068